CW00501033

The Little Book of Villains

The Little Book of Villains

First published in the UK by
New Internationalist Publications Ltd., Oxford, England.

The Little Book of Villains
Compilation © Troth Wells/New Internationalist 2001
All rights reserved. No part of this publication may be reproduced,
transmitted or stored in a retrieval system, in any form or by any means,
without permission in writing from the publishers.

Printed on recycled paper by C&C Offset Printing Co. Ltd., Hong Kong.
Designed by Ian Nixon

British Library Cataloguing-in-Publication Data.
A catalogue record for this book is available from the British Library.

ISBN 1 869847 97 0

New Internationalist Publications Ltd.
Registered Office: 55 Rectory Road, Oxford OX4 1BW

www.newint.org

THE LITTLE BOOK OF Villains

Compiled by Troth Wells

Foreword

Vitriolic, venomous, vituperative or just plain vile, the villains in this little book will make your hair curl – or have you seething with rage – or even laughing at some of their absurdities. Read their words, from Roman emperor Caligula down to Hitler, Mussolini and Stalin and recent tyrants such as Idi Amin, Pinochet and Suharto – not to mention Ronald Reagan, Maggie Thatcher and the scourge of the liberal world, George W Bush, plus some controversial characters like Eminem and Marilyn Manson. Through their own words, you can see just what makes the villains tick!

From the horse's mouth

People that are really very weird can get into sensitive positions and have a tremendous impact on history.

George W Bush (b. 1946) US president since 2000.

Might of the right

I truly believe in the goodness of
American power. [All nations will]
either organize with us or against us. But
we are the organizing principle.

Madeleine Albright (b. 1937) US secretary of state.

Capitalism

This American system of ours, call it Americanism, call it capitalism, call it what you will, gives each and every one of us a great opportunity if we only seize it with both hands and make the most of it.

Al Capone (1899-1947) US mafia leader.

Doing well is the result of doing good. That's what capitalism is all about.

Adnan Kashoggi, Saudi arms dealer.

Of course...

I am only concerned about the needless anxieties which the programme may cause to pensioners in our group.

Robert Maxwell (1923-1991) UK media magnate, explaining to *Mirror* readers why he issued a writ banning BBC TV from screening a programme about his illegal use of pension funds, 1991.

Fair deal

Deals work best when each side gets something it wants from the other.

Donald Trump (b. 1946)
US billionaire entrepreneur.

Taxing topic

They can't collect legal taxes from illegal money.

Al Capone (1899-1947) US mafia leader.

The taxpayer – that's someone who works for the federal government but doesn't have to take the civil service examination.

Ronald Reagan (b. 1911) US president 1980-88.

Muscle men

I will observe the constitution whenever it does not contradict military decrees.

> **Colonel Hugo Banzer**, US-backed president of Bolivia 1971-1978 and from 1999.

Our regime is based on bayonets and blood, not on hypocritical elections.

> **General Francisco Franco** (1892-1975) Spanish fascist leader 1939-75.

We are no longer interested in elections except as a means to reach our objectives.

> **Juán D Peron** (1895-1974) Argentinian president 1946-55, and 1973-4, on his return to power in 1973.

Cut and thrust

*W*hy are people saying we shouldn't export trees? What do we grow forests for? To cut 'em down and sell 'em!

Michael Moore, director-general of the World Trade Organization.

*E*thical decisions that injure a firm's ability to compete are actually immoral.

Helmut Maucher, former Nestlé chief executive. Nestlé was one of the companies pushing the sale of infant formula to developing countries in situations where it could not be prepared safely.

Fascist faith

Fascism is a religion; the twentieth century will be known in history as the century of fascism.

Benito Mussolini (1883-1945) Italian fascist leader 1925-43.

Em's way

Follow me and do exactly what the song says/
Smoke weed, take pills, drop outta school/
Kill people and drink.

Eminem/Marshall Mathers (b. 1972) US rap musician.

Vichy business

To make a union with Great Britain would be fusion with a corpse.

Marshal Pétain (1856-1951) French leader, declining British premier Winston Churchill's offer of political union against Nazi Germany. When Germany invaded France, Pétain led the collaborationist administration in Vichy.

Gun lobby

It is time [youth] found out that the politically correct doctrine of today has misled them. And that when they reach legal age, if they do not break our laws, they have a right to choose to own a gun – a handgun, a long gun, a small gun, a large gun, a black gun, a purple gun, a pretty gun, an ugly gun – and to use that gun to defend themselves and their loved ones or to engage in any lawful purpose they desire without apology or explanation to anyone, ever.

Charlton Heston (b. 1923) US actor and president of the National Rifle Association which opposes any form of gun control.

You won't get gun control by disarming law-abiding citizens. There's only one way to get real gun control: disarm the thugs and the criminals, lock them up, and if you don't actually throw away the key, at least lose it for a long time.

Ronald Reagan (b. 1911) US president
1980-88, in 1983.

Unfair advantage

Unfortunately we wear uniforms and the criminals always spot us.

Francisco Luna, a Mexico City police chief, in 1998.

Killing two birds

We hope to wipe out drug traffic in Argentina. The guerrillas are the main drug users in Argentina. Therefore, this anti-drug campaign will automatically be an anti-guerrilla campaign as well.

Jose Lopez Rega, Argentinian minister, at the signing of the US-Argentina anti-drug treaty in 1976.

Read my lips

U ndoubtedly, we shall have no further need of resorting to the method of mass purges.

Joseph Stalin (1879-1953) Soviet leader 1929-53; he was planning another purge when he died.

N obody will be persecuted.

General Washington Carrasco, Chilean military official, after the 1973 coup that deposed President Salvador Allende. Allende was killed along with many other Chileans; thousands more were tortured.

PR tip

Put your words in someone else's mouth.

Merrill Rose, executive vice-president of PR firm Porter/Novelli.

Blood on their hands

*I*n the space of two hours, all [Atahualpa's] troops were annihilated... six or seven thousand Indians lay dead and many more had their arms cut off.

> Contemporary Spanish account of the capture of Atahualpa, the Inca (leader) of Peru, 1532. Atahualpa was later killed by conquistador Francisco Pizarro.

*B*lood alone moves the wheels of history.

> **Benito Mussolini** (1883-1945) Italian fascist leader 1925-43.

Formula One

You treat a woman like a car because it is a very highly strung and nervous piece of equipment. You have to coax it sometimes to get the best out of it, you have to correct it and treat it gently, and at times, maybe on a difficult circuit, you have to give it a really good thrashing because that is the only thing it understands.

Jackie Stewart (b. 1939) British racing driver
1965-1973, in 1969.

Presidential puissance

We are all the President's men.

Henry Kissinger (b. 1923) US national security adviser 1969-73; secretary of state 1973-77. Deeply involved in the Nixon administrations 1968-74.

When the President does it, that means it is not illegal.

Richard Nixon (1913-1994) US president 1968-74; forced from office in 1974 after the Watergate scandal and White House cover-up of a break-in to the Democratic Party campaign headquarters.

Zapping investment

While Chiapas does not pose a fundamental threat to Mexican political stability, it is perceived to do so by many in the investment community. The government will need to eliminate the Zapatistas to demonstrate their effective control of the national territory and security policy.

US Chase Bank, in 1995, after the indigenous peoples' Zapatista uprising in Chiapas, Mexico the previous year.

Hawkish sentiments

You should read the Koran. You'll see what Arabs think about the Jews. They want to take this land by violence.

Ariel Sharon (b. 1928) Israeli prime minister since 2001. He was implicated by the official Israeli Kahan Commission for his role in the massacre at the Sabra and Shatilla Palestinian refugee camps in 1982. Under the principles of the Fourth Geneva Convention Sharon is a war criminal responsible for the massacre of nearly 3,000 Arab civilians.

On top

I try to keep in touch with the details... I also look at the product daily. That doesn't mean you interfere, but it's important occasionally to show the ability to be involved. It shows you understand what's happening.

Rupert Murdoch (b. 1931) Australian-born media magnate, currently No. 22 in *Fortune* magazine's richest people list.

Ouch!

We do not have a policy of scorched earth. We have a policy of scorched Communists.

General Ephrain Rios Montt, military ruler of Guatemala 1982-83, on the success of the 'beans and bullets' counter-insurgency programme, 1980s.

Bob's mantra

I have no intention of making anyone redundant. I will never interfere with editorial freedom. Union recognition will continue.

Robert Maxwell (1923-1991) UK media magnate, on acquiring *The Daily Mirror* in 1984. Maxwell's sackings were legion and he constantly intervened on editorial matters.

Mad minister

Nobody need be worried about BSE [mad cow disease] in this country or anywhere else in the world.

John Gummer (b. 1939) British minister of agriculture, in 1990. By 1996 167,000 cases had arisen; thousands of cattle had to be slaughtered, and a human form of the disease began to claim victims.

Murderous women

M y husbands have been very unlucky.

> **Lucrezia Borgia** (1480-1519) Italian noble,
> thought to have murdered her husbands.

U nsex me here/And fill me from
the crown to the toe top full/Of
direst cruelty.

> **Lady Macbeth**, character in Shakespeare's
> play *Macbeth*.

White man's land

The outside world and especially the warmongering leaders on the African continent must understand that the white man in South Africa is not expendable. Let them make decisions at the UN or other world bodies; those decisions will not wipe the white man off the face of Africa because we, the people of South Africa – and here I am speaking on behalf of the Whites – are here to stay. Let nobody mistake it. Let them spit as much fire as they want about the so-called immorality of the apartheid policy. We in South Africa know that it is the only feasible policy.

B John Vorster (1915-1983) South African nationalist leader 1966-78, in 1966.

We are in Africa because it is our right, our duty and our interest. But we are in Africa because that is also the general interest of the free world.

Alberto Franco Noguira, Portuguese foreign minister, in 1968, when Portugal's empire included Mozambique, Angola and Guinea plus East Timor in the Pacific.

Toys for the boys

A slipping gear could let your M203 grenade-launcher fire when you least expect it. That would make you quite unpopular in what's left of your unit.

PS Magazine, US military periodical, in 1993.

Backing the brutes

[Idi Amin] is a welcome contrast to other African leaders and a staunch friend of Britain.

> *The Daily Telegraph*, in 1971. Amin's coup in 1971 brought him to power in Uganda where his brutal rule continued until 1979.

The hour of truth has come. Today England recognised us. Tomorrow it will be the whole world.

> **General Francisco Franco** (1892-1975) Spanish fascist leader 1939-1975, in March 1939 at the start of his regime.

Dam people

OK, I got the point that we should not displace people. Then do not construct the dams!

S C Varma, chair of the Narmada Valley Development Authority in India, in 1987. The dam construction has displaced hundreds of thousands of people.

Male violence

It is beyond question that [men] have the right to establish laws which will force a woman to yield to the ardours of him who desires her; violence itself being one of the results of this right... Has not Nature proved to [men] that we have this right, by allotting us the strength necessary to force [women] to our desires?

Marquis de Sade (1714-1814) French writer, in *La Philosophie dans le Boudoir*, 1795.

Freudian failure

The great question that has never been answered and which I have not yet been able to answer, despite my thirty years of research into the feminine soul, is 'What does a woman want?'

Sigmund Freud (1856-1939) German psychoanalyst.

Joe's maxim

Gratitude is a sickness suffered by dogs.

Joseph Stalin (1879-1953) Soviet leader 1929-53.

Hateful thoughts

The Arab is a fatalist; the southern Italian is emotionally unstable; the Japanese and French are philosophical; and the Scandinavian is boring.

Hendrick Verwoerd (1901-1966) South African nationalist leader 1958-66.

Would that the Roman people had but one neck!

Caligula (Gaius Caesar 12-41 AD) Roman emperor, infamous for his brutality.

The State, not only as a sovereign of semi-barbaric populations but also as a depository of social authority should have no scruples in obliging and if necessary forcing these rude Negroes in Africa, these ignorant Pariahs in Asia, these half-witted savages from Oceania, to work.

António Enes, Portuguese colonial administrator, in the 1890s.

All those who are not racially pure are mere chaff.

Adolf Hitler (1889-1945) German Nazi leader 1933-45.

Homophobe

[Gays are] worse than dogs and pigs; a colonial invention, unknown in African tradition.

Robert Mugabe (b. 1924) President of Zimbabwe since 1980. Gays and lesbians are second only to white farmers on the hitlist of scapegoats he uses to divert attention from the ailing, corrupt state of his country.

Greed

Greed is all right, by the way. I think greed is healthy. You can be greedy and still feel good about yourself.

> **Ivan F Boesky** (b. 1937) US investment banker jailed for illegal insider trading.

The point is that you can't be too greedy.

> **Donald Trump** (b. 1946) US entrepreneur.

War-mongering

In Indo-China we have allied ourselves to the desperate effort of the French régime to hang on to the remnants of an empire.

John F Kennedy (1917-1963) US president 1961-3, in 1951. The US became involved in Vietnam to fight communism after the French were defeated in 1954.

I was told by [US Defense Secretary] McNamara that I should ask for the troops I needed to bring about the end result. I should not worry about public opinion. I should not worry about the economy. I should not even concern myself as to the availability of the troops.

General William Westmoreland (b. 1914) US commander in Vietnam, in 1965.

Do not overlook the possibility that in order to defeat the guerrilla you may have to resort to a scorched earth policy... [Have] plenty of artillery, for the Oriental greatly fears artillery.

General Douglas MacArthur (1880-1964), advice to General Westmoreland on the Vietnam war.

Or, put another way

I didn't just screw Ho Chi Minh. I cut his pecker off.

Lyndon Johnson (1908-1973) US president 1963-68, on the US bombing of Hanoi, North Vietnam, in 1964. Ho Chi Minh was the leader of North Vietnam.

Sticky fingers

If you want to steal, steal a little cleverly, in a nice way. If you steal so much as to become rich overnight, you will be caught.

Mobutu Sese Seko (1930-1997) dictator of Zaire (now DR Congo) 1965-97, in 1976. He stole an estimated $5 billion from his country.

Spinning a web

This was an operational error and not the result of any issue with Microsoft or third-party products, nor with the security of our networks.

Adam Sohn, Microsoft spokesperson, after the software giant's web sites were largely unreachable due to a bad network design, 2001.

Sex object

I have no actual claim to the possession of such and such a woman, but I have an incontestable one to the enjoyment of her; and I have a right to force her to this enjoyment if she refuses me.

Marquis de Sade (1740-1814) French writer, in *La Philosophie dans le Boudoir*, 1795.

Crusading words

If one permits an infidel to continue in his role as a corrupter of the earth, his moral suffering will be all the worse. If one kills the infidel, and this stops him from perpetrating his misdeeds, his death will be a blessing to him.

Ayatollah Khomeini (1900-1989) Iranian religious and political leader 1979-89.

X-rated

I've always thought that the most extraordinary special effect you could do is to buy a child at the moment of its birth, sit it on a little chair and say, 'You'll have three score years and ten,' and take a photograph every minute. 'And we'll watch you and photograph you for ten years after you die, then we'll run the film.' Wouldn't that be extraordinary? We'd watch this thing get bigger and bigger, and flower to become extraordinary and beautiful, then watch it crumble, decay, and rot.

Clive Barker (b. 1952) British writer and horror movie director.

Ariel view

I believe in peace, but I believe in peace that might provide Israel with real security for its existence.

Ariel Sharon (b. 1928) Israeli prime minister since 2001. He was implicated by the official Israeli Kahan Commission for his role in the massacre at the Sabra and Shatilla Palestinian refugee camps in 1982. Under the principles of the Fourth Geneva Convention Sharon is a war criminal responsible for the massacre of nearly 3,000 Arab civilians.

Single-minded

I shall be an autocrat: that's my trade.
And the good Lord will forgive me:
that's his.

Catherine the Great (1729-1796) Empress of Russia.

I am extraordinarily patient, provided I
get my own way in the end.

Margaret Thatcher (b. 1925) British
prime minister 1979-90.

Gay stance

Although the particular inclination of the homosexual person is not a sin, it is a more or less strong tendency ordered toward an intrinsic moral evil; and thus the inclination itself must be seen as an objective disorder. Therefore special concern and pastoral attention should be directed toward those who have this condition, lest they be led to believe that the living out of this orientation in homosexual activity is a morally acceptable option. It is not.

Pope John-Paul II (b. 1920), in 1986.

This sort of thing may be tolerated by the French, but we are British – thank God.

Lord Montgomery (1887-1976) British field marshal, about a bill to relax laws on homosexuality, in 1965.

God-given

I f you want to make a million, the quickest way is to start your own religion.

L Ron Hubbard (1911-1986) founder of Scientology.

J esus Christ is trying to follow me, my footsteps, all the way.

Sun Myung Moon (b. 1920) leader of the Unification Church (the 'Moonies').

Chic poverty

I did not feel 'evil' when I wrote advertisements for Puerto Rico. They helped attract industry and tourists to a country which had been living on the edge of starvation for 400 years.

David Ogilvy, of the Ogilvy advertising agency, in 1985.

Ways of seeing

Before the organization of the Blackshirt [fascist] movement, free speech did not exist in this country.

> **Oswald Mosley** (1896-1980) British politician and founder of the British Union of Fascists.

Throughout my political life I have never had double agendas. I have never spoken out of both sides of my mouth.

> **Mangosuthu Buthelezi** (b. 1928) South African homeland leader, in 1985; supporter of the apartheid regime's 'Bantustans' for black South Africans.

I am not and never have been, a man of the right. My position was on the left and is now in the centre of politics.

Oswald Mosley (1896-1980) British politician and founder of the British Union of Fascists.

I am not beating it. I am encouraging it with a stick.

Mary Chipperfield, of the Chipperfield circus, on a video showing her beating a camel at her training centre, in 1998.

Hidden meaning

Laos wasn't the center of activity and since we didn't wish to get the US forces directly involved in a confrontation there while the confrontation was being pursued in South Vietnam, it was decided not to take an overt cognizance of this breakdown [of neutrality], and to continue to operate in a covert way.

William Sullivan, US ambassador to Laos 1964-68.

You do not reform a world by ignoring it.

George Bush (b. 1924) US president 1988-92.

With the People

The central cardinal element of His Majesty's style of government is *Sentiasa Bersama Rakyat* or 'Always Together With His Subjects', which is testimony of a living democracy and good governance in the context of the daily lives of Bruneians.

Sultan of Brunei's office. Bruneians have not been allowed to vote since 1962.

Iraq needs a symbol far more than [other countries] because the state of development is new and the state of backwardness is deep, and because there are in Iraq various religions, sects and ethnicities. Saddam must therefore be shared by all of them.

Saddam Hussain (b. 1937), Iraqi president, in 1984.

Kinky

I think that's a very kinky issue with the panties and bras. That's the thing that they will display: shoes, panties and bras.

Imelda Marcos (b. 1929) 'First Lady' of corrupt Philippines' president Ferdinand Marcos; on the exhibition of thousands of pairs of shoes and other articles of clothing left behind when she and her husband fled the Philippines, 1986.

Grown-up talk

The most dangerous thing about student riots is that adults take them seriously.

Georges Pompidou (1911-1974) French president 1969-74, after the student demonstrations of 1968.

Death sentence

I believe that people would be alive today if there were a death penalty.

Nancy Reagan (b. 1921) US 'First Lady' 1980-88.

Criminals should not be tried; they should be killed.

Ayatollah Khomeini (1900-1989) Iranian religious and political leader 1979-89.

The author of the *Satanic Verses* book, which is against Islam, the Prophet and the Koran, and all those involved in its publication who were aware of its content, are sentenced to death. I ask all Moslems to execute them wherever they find them.

Ayatollah Khomeini (1900-1989) Iranian religious and political leader 1979-89.

Explanations 1

The takeover was intended to save all Chileans, not to benefit just a few. The best defenders of the underprivileged classes, of the poor folks of our society, are the four members of the Junta, who always try to favor the needy classes when considering any initiative, whether it concerns salaries or agrarian reform.

General Augusto Lutz, secretary of the Chilean junta, after the 1973 military coup which toppled the elected president, Salvador Allende. Allende was killed, as were many other Chileans; thousands were tortured.

I characterise the policy of apartheid as a policy of growth from its own roots, from its own institutions and from its own power. That is the policy of slow development; by means of mother-tongue and by means of environmental education to make literate and useful people of [black South Africans] within their own circle.

Hendrick Verwoerd (1901-1966) South African nationalist leader 1958-66, in 1965.

Cynic's view

All universal moral principles are idle
fancies.

Marquis de Sade (1740-1814) French writer.

Thinking big

If a woman like Eva Peron with no ideals can get that far, think how far I can go with all the ideals that I have.

> **Margaret Thatcher** (b. 1925) British prime minister 1979-1990, in 1980. Eva 'Evita' Peron was involved in Argentinian politics.

My life was too short to achieve the conquest of the whole world.

> **Genghis Khan**, 13th century Mongol expansionist.

Wriggling

It's a lie. If they don't have proof and facts to back it up, it is slander and defamation. Honestly, that's more cruel than murder.

Kemusu Argamulja Suharto (b. 1921) President of Indonesia 1967-99, when *Time* magazine published an investigation into his family's wealth.

I think it's the mark of a great player to be confident in tough situations.

John McEnroe (b. 1959) US tennis player famous for vitriolic attacks on players and umpires.

Spinning words

It would not be impossible to prove, with sufficient repetition and psychological understanding of the people concerned, that a square is in fact a circle. They are mere words and words can be moulded until they clothe ideas in disguise.

Joseph Goebbels (1897-1945) German Nazi
minister of propaganda 1933-45.

Environmental lobby

Right now the environment movement is a perfect bogeyman for us. In order to get people to join and donate money [to us] we need opposition.

Alan Gottlieb, US Center for the Defense of Free Enterprise, in the 1990s.

It isn't pollution that's harming the environment. It's the impurities in our air and water that are doing it.

George W Bush (b. 1946) US president since 2000.

I've always thought that under-populated countries in Africa are vastly under-polluted, their air quality is probably vastly inefficiently low compared to Los Angeles or Mexico City.

Lawrence H Summers (b. 1954) former chief economist at the World Bank, in 1991.

The Ford engineering staff, although mindful that automobile engines produce exhaust gases, feels these waste vapours are dissipated in the atmosphere quickly and do not present an air pollution problem.

Dan J Chabek, Ford spokesperson, in 1953.

Clear conscience

I came to carry out the struggle, not to kill people. My conscience is clear. As I told you before, they fought against us, so we had to take measures to defend ourselves.

Pol Pot (1928-1998) Cambodian dictator 1975-79, defending his Khmer Rouge regime which had killed some two million Cambodians in that period.

Forget the losers...

Globalization is already a success. There will always be losers, like everywhere in life, but globalization is almost win-win.

Helmut Maucher, former Nestlé chief executive, in 1998. Nestlé was one of the companies pushing the sale of infant formula to developing countries in situations where it could not be prepared safely.

To some extent, if you've seen one city slum you've seen them all.

Spiro Agnew (1918-1996) US vice-president 1968-72, in 1968.

Here to help

The Soviet Army was invited to protect the sovereignty of the People's Republic of Czechoslovakia.

Leonid Brezhnev (1906-1982) Soviet leader 1977-82, after the invasion of Czechoslovakia in 1968.

Chairman Mao ZeDong of the Central People's Government and commander-in-chief Chu Teh of the People's Liberation Army are deeply concerned about the prolonged oppression of the Tibetan people by British and American imperialism and by Chiang Kai-shek's reactionary government and have accordingly ordered their Army to move into Tibet to help the Tibetan people shake off this oppression forever.

Xinhua (New China News Agency), in November 1950.

Opportunity knocks

This is virgin territory for whorehouses.

Al Capone (1899-1947) Italian-born
US mafia leader, about Chicago.

Hard men

Pity is treason.

> **Maximilien Robespierre** (1758-1794)
> French revolutionary.

May God have mercy upon my enemies, because I won't.

> **George S Patton Jr** (1885-1945) feisty US general.

The duty of the men at Stalingrad is to be dead.

> **Adolf Hitler** (1889-1945)
> German Nazi leader 1933-45.

One-party state

*W*hile we work seriously to achieve our central slogan – 'if we win the youth we will win the future' – we should achieve other objectives, namely to eradicate the roots of other political movements.

Saddam Hussain (b. 1937) Iraqi president
since 1979, in 1976.

Rap attack

They attack Eminem 'cause I rap this way/But I'm glad 'cause they feed me the fuel I need for the fire to burn.

Eminem/Marshall Mathers (b. 1972) US rap musician.

In for a penny...

We are for aiding our allies by sharing some of our material blessings with those nations which share in our fundamental beliefs, but we are against doling out money government to government, creating bureaucracy, if not socialism, all over the world. We set out to help 19 countries. We are helping 107. We spent $146 billion. With that money, we bought a 2-million-dollar yacht for Haile Selassie. We bought dress suits for Greek undertakers, extra wives for Kenya government officials. We bought a thousand TV sets for a place where they have no electricity.

Ronald Reagan (b. 1911) US president 1980-88.

The heart bleeds...

Aid is given under such conditions that its use is really decided by the Americans and not by us. Decisions like how many planes or helicopters we buy, how we spend our money, how many trucks we need, how many bullets... and where our priorities should be – all of that is decided by the one who gives the money [the US].

José Napoleón Duarte, US-backed president of El Salvador, in 1984.

Plain speaking

I am free of all prejudices. I hate everyone equally.

W C Fields (1879-1948) US actor.

Explanations 2

Our movement took a grip on cowardly Marxism and from it extracted the meaning of socialism. It also took from the cowardly middle-class parties their nationalism. Throwing both into the cauldron of our way of life there emerged, as clear as a crystal, the synthesis – German National Socialism.

Hermann Goering (1893-1946) German Nazi gestapo (secret police) head.

The keystone of the fascist doctrine is its conception of the State, of its essence, its functions and its aims. For fascism, the State is absolute, individuals and groups relative.

Benito Mussolini (1883-1945) Italian fascist leader 1922-43.

Breathing space

[A ruler] should consider peace only as a breathing-time, which gives him leisure to contrive, and furnishes his ability to execute, military plans.

Niccolò Machiavelli (1469-1527) Italian politician; author of *The Prince* in which his apparent support of devious rulers brought the term *machiavellian* into politics.

Land of the free

Traditional authoritarian governments... are more compatible with US interests.

> **Jeanne Kirkpatrick** (b. 1926) US ambassador to the UN 1981-85, in 1979.

I saved the country from the abyss.

> **General Saw Maung**, chairman of the State Law and Order Restoration Council (SLORC) regime in Burma, on the failed CPB (communist party) bid for power, in 1988. SLORC, now the State Peace and Development Council, has kept democracy leader Aung San Suu Kyi under house arrest since she won the election in 1990.

Women's place

A society in which women are taught anything at all but the management of a family, the care of men and the creation of the future generation is a society which is on the way out.

L Ron Hubbard (1911-1986) founder of Scientology, in 1980.

When a woman becomes a scholar there is usually something wrong with her sex organs.

Friedrich Nietzsche (1844-1900) German philosopher.

Let the woman learn in silence with all subjection. But I suffer not a woman to teach, nor to usurp authority over the man, but to be in silence.

St Paul (c. 64 AD) Christian apostle.

Global grasp

Our reach is unmatched around the world. We're reaching people from the moment they wake up until they fall asleep.

Rupert Murdoch (b. 1931) Australian-born head of News Corp which uses its global reach to localize its tax payments, getting its accounts done in low-tax countries.

A bad patch

There is a great expectation in our country – around the land which is still to come to our people in a big way; and around the economy which is going through a bad patch.

Robert Mugabe (b. 1924) President of Zimbabwe since 1980. White farmers are on the hitlist of scapegoats he uses to divert attention from the ailing, corrupt state of his country.

Missile mission

We're not building missiles to fight a war. We're building missiles to preserve the peace.

Ronald Reagan (b. 1911) US president 1980-88.

Fired up

I never made an inflammatory statement in my life.

The Revd Ian Paisley (b. 1926)
Northern Ireland politician.

*N*o surrender!

The Revd Ian Paisley (b. 1926)
Northern Ireland politician.

Personality cultures

After this political act [referendum] there will never again be an election to elect a chief of state on the soil of Haiti... I shall be lord and master. I have always talked with the wild energy, the savagery which characterizes me.

François ('Papa Doc') Duvalier (1907-1971) President-for-life of Haiti 1957-71, in 1964.

People of Haiti, I am the heir to the political philosophy, the doctrine and the revolution which my late father incarnated as president-for-life [and] I have decided to continue his work with the same fierce energy and the same intransigence.

Jean-Claude ('Baby Doc') Duvalier (b. 1952) President-for-life of Haiti 1971-86, in 1971 when assuming the presidency after his father's death. He was overthrown in 1986 and went into exile.

Genocidal tendencies

In some countries, genocide is not really important.

François Mitterand (1916-1996) French president, on the massacre of nearly a million Tutsis by Hutus in Rwanda in 1994.

Genocide is a natural phenomenon. Genocide is not only permitted, it is recommended, even commanded by the word of the Almighty, whenever it is useful for the survival or restoration of the kingdom of the chosen nation, or for the preservation and spreading of its one and only correct faith.

Franjo Tudjman (1922-1999) President of Croatia 1990-1999, in 1997. Tudjman presided over the crushing of Serb opposition in Krajina in 1995, considered one of the biggest ethnic cleansing operations in former Yugoslavia's wars.

By continuing the deportation of the [Armenian] orphans to their destinations during the intense cold, we are ensuring their eternal rest.

Talaat Pasha (1874-1921) Ottoman Turkish minister of the interior and main architect of the genocide of 600,000 Armenians in 1915.

To sum it all up, I must say that I regret nothing.

Adolf Eichmann (1906-1962) German Nazi secret police head, responsible for sending millions of Jews to their deaths. He was convicted and hanged in Israel.

Music to the ears

MTV is associated with the forces of freedom and democracy around the world.

> **Sumner Redstone** (b. 1923) owner of MTV music channel, in 1994.

The Central Intelligence Agency owns everyone of any significance in the major media.

> **William Colby** (1920-1996) director of the US CIA.

Black and white

As I look ahead, I am filled with foreboding. Like the Roman, I seem to see 'the River Tiber foaming with much blood'.

Enoch Powell (1912-1998) UK politician, with his view on the effects of immigration.

Most boarding houses here are not large enough to take coloured and white guests at the same time.

Mrs D Brookes, UK Withernsea Landladies' Association, in the 1960s.

I ain't going to let no darkies and white folk segregate together in this town.

Eugene Connor, police commissioner for Birmingham, Alabama, in the US in 1950.

Leaders of the western world

Hawaii has always been a very pivotal role in the Pacific. It is in the Pacific. It is part of the US that is an island that is right here.

Dan Quayle (b. 1947) US vice-president 1988-92, in 1992.

I stand by all the misstatements that I've made.

George W Bush (b. 1946) US president since 2000, in 1993.

The United States has much to offer the Third World War.

Ronald Reagan (b. 1911) US president 1980-88, in 1975.

There is no Soviet domination of Eastern Europe and there never will be under a Ford administration.

Gerald Ford (b. 1909) US president 1974-76, in 1976. At the time, the USSR held sway over Poland, Hungary, Romania, Bulgaria, Czechoslovakia and East Germany.

Barrier method

You must not wear condoms. They do not stop disease. Anyone who tells you otherwise is a liar. They are designed to stop us breeding.

Winnie Madikizela Mandela (b. 1934) South African politician, in 1998.

Serbian might

We shall win despite the fact that Serbia's enemies outside the country are plotting against it, along with those in the country. We tell them that we enter every battle with the aim of winning it.

Slobodan Milosevic (b. 1941) President of Serbia 1990-2000; President of Yugoslavia 1997-2000; during his 1988 rise to supreme power in Serbia, telling supporters that Serbia would win the battle for Kosovo. He was deposed in the 2000 elections, and is wanted by Interpol for crimes against humanity.

Trump card

As long as you're going to think anyway, think big.

Donald Trump (b. 1946) US billionaire entrepreneur.

Weasel words

It is not a bomb. It is a device which is exploding.

Jacques le Blanc, French ambassador to New Zealand, on the French nuclear tests in the Pacific, 1995. In 1985, French secret service agents blew up a Greenpeace ship which had been protesting against the tests, killing two activists.

We have not conducted [nuclear] tests in a way which is hazardous to health.

Dr Willard Libby, US Atomic Energy Commission, in 1957.

Bosom pals

I don't see why we need to stand by and watch a country go communist because of the irresponsibility of its own people.

> **Henry Kissinger** (b. 1923) US politician, prior to Pinochet's US-backed coup against Chile's democratically-elected president Salvador Allende in 1973.

I believe that the time to act is near.

> **General Augusto Pinochet** (b. 1915), two days before the 1973 US-supported coup in which President Salvador Allende of Chile was overthrown and killed.

Shah power

Nobody can overthrow me. I have the support of 700,000 troops, all the workers, and most of the people. I have the power.

Mohammed Reza Pahlavi (1919-1980) Shah of Iran 1941-79, a year before the 1979 revolution that overthrew him.

American Indians

The nobility of the Redskin is extinguished, and what few are left are a pack of whining curs who lick the hand that smites them. The Whites, by law of conquest, by justice of civilization, are masters of the American continent, and the best safety of the frontier settlements will be secured by the total annihilation of the few remaining Indians. Why not annihilation? Their glory has fled, their spirit broken, their manhood effaced; better that they should die than live the miserable wretches that they are.

L Frank Baum (1856-1919) author of *The Wizard of Oz*, shortly before the Wounded Knee massacre in 1890.

The Army is the Indians' best friend.
George Custer (1839-1876) US general, in 1870;
Custer was the army's foremost Indian slayer.

I don't feel we did wrong in taking this great country away from [Indians]. There were great numbers of people who needed new land, and the Indians were selfishly trying to keep it for themselves.

John Wayne (1907-1979) US actor.

Attacking their own

I have a list of 205 people that were known to the Secretary of State as being members of the Communist Party and who, nevertheless, are still working and shaping policy in the State Department.

Joseph McCarthy (1908-1957) US politician and chair of the Senate Investigations Subcommittee into supposed communist infiltration, in 1950.

We have no political prisoners – only Communists and others involved in conspiracies against the country.

Park Chung Hee (1917-1979) President of
South Korea 1963-79, in 1974.

There can be no fifty-fifty Americanism in this country. There is room here for only 100 per cent Americanism, only for those who are Americans and nothing else.

Theodore Roosevelt (1858-1919)
US president 1901-09, in 1918.

Sick joker

We were told four years ago that 17 million people went to bed hungry every night. Well, that was probably true. They were all on a diet.

Ronald Reagan (b. 1911) US president 1980-88, in 1964.

Letting the weeds grow

It has been said that children should be kept at school until 14 years of age; but the amount of labour which lads between 10 and 14 can perform should not be ignored. Since the present educational system has come into operation, the weeds have very much multiplied in Norfolk which was once regarded as quite the garden of England, weeding being particularly the work of children.

Earl Fortesque, English aristocrat, in 1880.

Some hope

I just hope [WTO critics] are as reasonable as we try to be and that we engage in an intellectual, democratic way without any media terrorism.

Michael Moore, director-general of the World Trade Organization.

Tactics

There is no avoiding war; it can only be postponed to the advantage of others.

Niccolò Machiavelli (1469-1527) Italian politician; author of *The Prince* in which his apparent support of devious rulers brought the term *machiavellian* into politics.

Never interrupt your enemy when he is making a mistake.

Napoleon Bonaparte (1769-1821) French emperor.

Sponsored crocs

Since the crocodile is the symbol of Lacoste, we thought they might be interested in sponsoring our crocodiles.

Silvino Gomes, commercial director
of Portugal's Lisbon Zoo, in 1998.

Licence to kill

In all my years in the Army I was never taught that communists were human beings. We were there to kill ideology carried by... pawns, blobs of flesh. I was there to destroy communism. We never conceived of people, men, women, children, babies.

Lt William Calley, US soldier, speaking of his part in the 1968 My Lai massacre in the US-Vietnam war.

Smokescreen

I'll tell you why I like the cigarette business. It costs a penny to make. Sell it for a dollar. It's addictive. And there's fantastic brand loyalty.

Warren Buffet (b. 1930) chief of US investment company Berkshire Hathaway.

Good guys and bad guys

When I was coming up, it was a dangerous world, and you knew exactly who they were. It was us versus them, and it was clear who them was. Today, we are not so sure who the they are, but we know they're there.

George W Bush (b. 1946) US president since 2000.

Perish the thought

Ideas are far more powerful than guns. We don't allow our enemies to have guns, why should we allow them to have ideas?

Joseph Stalin (1879-1953) Soviet leader 1929-53.

Adman's blues

As long as media was mass – when the consumer had no choice, when it was networks – you could fuck the consumer all day long with "ring around the collar" [soap powder ads], because she had to get up and turn off the set to avoid it. With cable and interactive sets, with that remote control, you can't do that. It's got to be the polite invitation, instead of the harangue.

Don Pepper, head of worldwide new business for US Chiat/Day PR company, in 1993.

Hustler

I'm really very, very disappointed that I didn't move into the retail business years ago, because I never realized the marketing power of the *Hustler* name and logo.

Larry Flynt, owner of *Hustler* men's magazine, in 1999.

Bullyboy

Somebody hits me, I'm going to hit him back. Even if it does look like he hasn't eaten in a while.

> **Charles Barkley** (b. 1963) US basketball star, after blatantly elbowing an Angolan opponent during the Olympics.

Butcher's view

As a butcher I deplore deliveries being carried into my shop from the high street on the neck of a van driver – especially if they are not wrapped. I can think of little more guaranteed to turn pedestrians off buying meat than the sight of pigs' heads flopping about as he struggles past them with the carcass.

Mr van der Laan, European butcher.

Sales talk

What good is the Moon? You can't buy it or sell it.

Ivan F Boesky (b. 1937) US investment banker,
jailed for illegal insider trading,

Sell your soul to yourself. You'll make more money.

Marilyn Manson/Brian Warner (b. 1959)
US rock star and self-styled satanist.

US achievement

Americans are achievers. They are obsessed with records of achievement in sports and they keep business achievement charts on their office walls and sports awards displayed in their homes.

United States Information Agency booklet
for foreign students, 1985.

Nobody gave a shit. Torturing [Viet Cong] prisoners was wholesale, rampant, at every level.

Don Dzagulones, US interrogator in Vietnam, in 1969.

Jackal speaks

My name is Illich Ramirez Sanchez. My profession is professional revolutionary. The world is my domain.

Illich Ramirez Sanchez/'Carlos the Jackal' (b. 1949)
Venezuelan mastermind of 1970s bombings/
killings around the world.

George the first

*W*hat's wrong with being a boring kind of guy?

George Bush (b. 1924) US president 1988-92.

Ice T-time

I got my 12-gauge [gun] sawed off
I got my headlights turned off
I'm about to bust some shots off
I'm about to dust some cops off.

Ice T (b. 1958) US rap musician.

Anti-feminist

The feminist agenda is not about equal rights for women. It is about a socialist, anti-family political movement that encourages women to leave their husbands, kill their children, practice witchcraft, destroy capitalism and become lesbians.

Pat Robertson (b. 1930) US evangelist.

A woman should be an illusion.

Ian Fleming (1908-1964) British novelist.

Straight talk

The buck stops with the guy who signs the checks.

Rupert Murdoch (b. 1931) Australian-born media
magnate, currently No. 22 in *Fortune*
magazine's richest people list.

We know best

You can see our respect for women by the fact that we have pledged to pay working women, even though they don't have to work.

Amir Khan Muttaqi, information minister for the Taliban, Afghanistan's Muslim fundamentalist regime. Women are forbidden to work in Afghanistan.

Coked up

A billion hours ago, human life appeared on earth. A billion minutes ago, Christianity emerged. A billion Coca-Colas ago was yesterday morning.

Coca-Cola company annual report, 1996.

Brash Branson

There are quite a few things I've done that even I thought might have been one step too far. But if you are willing to make a fool of yourself and make people smile, as long as you do it with a sense of fun, you can get away with it.

Richard Branson (b. 1950) boss of UK company Virgin whose activities include Virgin trains, one of the least reliable in the country.

Whiter than white

The President has kept all of the promises he intended to keep.

> **George Stephanopolous**, an aide to scandal-prone US president Bill Clinton.

There can be no whitewash at the White House.

> **Richard Nixon** (1913-1994) US president 1968-74. He was forced from office after the Watergate scandal and White House cover-up of the break-in to the Democratic Party campaign headquarters in 1972.

I don't think there is another person in America that wants to tell this story as much as I do.

> **Oliver L North**, former staff member of the US National Security Council, invoking Fifth Amendment against self-incrimination in the investigation into arms sales to Iran, 1986.

Dog fight

When I was first here, we had the advantages of the underdog. Now we have the disadvantages of the overdog.

Abba Eban (b. 1915) Israeli defence minister during the Six-Day War in 1967, after Israel repulsed Egyptian forces.

Colonial tool

Miscegenation is the most powerful force of colonial nationalism. Given equality to the European under the law and admitted to administrative, religious, political and military positions, the mulatto comes to adopt exclusively the customs and language of the conquering nation, and they constitute the most profitable and appropriate instrument for the spread of those ethnic characteristics in the native society.

Vaz de Sampiao e Melo, Portuguese official, in 1910.

Hidden depths

I have been underestimated for decades. I've done very well that way.

Helmut Kohl (b. 1930) German chancellor 1982-1998, in 1987 after an election victory. In 1999 he was suspected of accepting illegal funding for his CDU Party.

Truthful

I'm determined to give the blacks a fair crack of the whip.

Ian Smith (b. 1919) Prime Minister of Rhodesia (Zimbabwe) 1964-78, in 1972.

Dark side

From the world of darkness I did loose demons and devils in the power of scorpions to torment.

Charles Manson (b. 1934) US serial killer, from his unsuccessful plea for parole from life sentence for ritualistic murders, 1986.

A place to do business

There was no tragedy in Tiananmen [square]: there was no bloodbath. There is no change of China's policy. The open door remains open.

Li Peng (b. 1928) Chinese prime minister, after the violent repression of the pro-democracy movement in 1987.

Job losses

Our strategic plan in North America is to focus intensely on brand management, marketing and product design as a means to meet the casual clothing wants and needs of consumers. Shifting a significant portion of our manufacturing from the US and Canadian markets to contractors throughout the world will give the company greater flexibility to allocate resources and capital to its brands. These steps are crucial if we are to remain competitive.

John Ermatinger, of Levi Strauss, on the company's decision to shut down plants and lay off workers in 1997-99.

We're very focused on profitability and that's the light at the end of the tunnel for us.

Nirav Tolia, chief executive of US dot.com Epinions, on the company's sudden discovery that it didn't need 24 of its 88 employees, January 2001.

There is no such thing as Society. There are individual men and women, and there are families.

Margaret Thatcher (b. 1925) British prime minister 1979-90.

About New Internationalist Publications

New Internationalist is a publications co-operative based in Oxford,
UK, with editorial and sales offices in Aotearoa/New Zealand,
Australia and Canada. It publishes the **New Internationalist** magazine
on global issues, which has 65,000 subscribers worldwide. The NI also
produces the One World Calendar, Almanac and Greetings Cards,
and publications such as *Eye to Eye: Women* plus food books including
The Spices of Life and *Vegetarian Quick & Easy* – cooking from around
the world. New books from the **NI** include the *No-Nonsense Guide*
series, with titles including *Fair Trade*, *Climate Change* and *Globalization*.

For more information write to:

Aotearoa/New Zealand PO Box 4499, Christchurch.
newint@chch.planet.org.nz
Australia and PNG 28 Austin Street, Adelaide 5000, South Australia.
helenp@newint.com.au
Canada and US 1011 Bloor Street West, Toronto, Ontario M6H 1M1.
nican@web.net
United Kingdom 55 Rectory Road, Oxford OX4 1BW.
ni@newint.org

See all our products on the NI website at:
www.newint.org